The Three Bears

With REAL Photographs!

John Schwieder & Cindy Kumle

These photographs of the three bears were all taken over a two-week period on the coast of Katmai National Park in Alaska. We saw this mother and her cubs nearly every day during that time, sometimes for many hours. The bears taught me how normally solitary animals get along when they are in close proximity, how smart and tolerant of humans they are, how much cubs seem to love each other and want to touch—except when there's a fish—and just how hard bears have to work to survive.

I want to especially thank Steve Kaslowski, my companion on this trip. His commitment to his own work as a photographer has been an inspiration. Thanks to Sunny and Florian for being there also.

The wildness of Alaska grabbed me a long time ago. Photographs were instrumental. I'd see images of incredible wild places and I had to go there. Now I've come full circle by sharing my story with you.

Published by John Schwieder, Photographer
Anchorage, Alaska
www.johnschwieder.com
john@johnschwieder.com
Books and photographs available from the author.

©2010 by John Schwieder and Cindy Kumle
Edited by Susan Mitchell

Printed in China
Third Printing 2014

Rasmuson Library Cataloging in Publication Data
Schwieder, John.
   The three bears : with real photographs! / John Schwieder & Cindy Kumle. Anchorage, Alaska : John Schwieder, 2010.
p. cm.
ISBN: 978-0-9794874-2-2
1. Brown bear—Infancy—Alaska—Katmai National Park and Preserve—Juvenile literature—Pictorial works. 2. Katmai National Park and Preserve (Alaska)—Juvenile literature—Pictorial works.
I. Title. II. Kumle, Cindy.
QL737.C27 S385 2010

For my mom, Delores.
Because I'm one of three too.
    —John

For my family.
With their love and support I have become more adventurous.
    —Cindy

A new day begins on the wild coast of Katmai National Park in Alaska.

It's just getting light.

Fog still hangs in the valley.

The moon sinks slowly, soon to disappear over the mountains.

Salmon are here. They have just started swimming up the river.

Lots of bears have come from far and wide.

A mother bear has arrived with her three new cubs.

Today will be their first day fishing.

What an adventure they will have!

Katmai is one of eight major national parks in Alaska. The volcanic Aleutian mountain range rises as high as 7,000 feet from the coast. High mountain valleys contain large glaciers and active volcanos. On the east side, deep bays line the coast along Shelikof Strait. Katmai is well known for its high concentration of bears and fish. Normally bears are solitary except for moms and cubs, but when the fish are running, bears will tolerate other bears being close for a while.

The three bears arrive at the river bank.

The cubs have never crossed a river before.

They are wondering, "why has Mom brought us here?"

The cubs sit and wait. Should they really go?

All the bears pictured in this book are brown bears. Brown bears are the same type of bear as the grizzly bear. The only difference is where they live. Brown bears live on or near Alaska's coast. Grizzlies live in the state's interior. Alaska is also home to black bears and polar bears.

Mom is confident.

She knows the way.

Paw by paw, the cubs begin to follow, though somewhat hesitantly.

The three bears pause, lined up on the bank.
"Who will go first? Hmm...not me!"

Brown bears have long, strong claws for digging, holding on, and hunting bigger animals like moose and caribou. They can't use their claws for climbing trees like black bears. Black bears are smaller and have shorter, sharper claws.

Of the three bears,
there's a big one,
a middle one,
and a little one.

And the little one is a she.

"You go first," say the brother bears.

With a nudge and a push she's on her way.

The littlest bear is the adventurous one.

Adventure is just part of her spirit.

She sees Mom waiting for her on the other side.

That gives her confidence to lead her brothers across.

The brothers follow and all three bears
forge ahead together.

Across the river they go:
little bear behinds and little bare feet!

Mother bear waits patiently.

This is the first of many things she will teach them today,
making sure they are safe along the way.

Mother bears have a reputation for being fierce.
They are very protective of their cubs.
Cubs are pretty helpless for the first few years of life.
Dangers include adult male bears, wolves, and getting lost.

Finally Mom and the cubs arrive at the fishing hole.

They are not the first.

The three bears are hungry, but tension fills the air.

Mom gathers the cubs close.

Little One is ready to go.

Three other mothers with older cubs are already here.

"Where will we fish?" the three bears ask.

Mom looks for an open spot.

One to four cubs are born in the den in January. They are very little, weighing only about one pound. Bear cubs stay with their moms from two to five years before striking out on their own. Bears are considered adults when they are six years old.

Mother bear starts fishing, leaving the three in a pile.

Cubs like to be close and touch, especially today with all the new things.

All three wonder what they're learning now.

"Mom seems to be just standing there."

Quick as lightning, she makes a dash!

The three bears stand up all in a row to see
what Mom has caught.

Other bears are watching too.

Many more bears live near the coast of Alaska, compared to the
interior, simply because there is more for them to eat, especially
fish. When the fish runs are over, these bears will spread out to
an average of one per square mile, compared to one per hundred
square miles in parts of the state with less food for bears.

The cubs finally get their first taste of fish.

Of course they like to eat it—and for bears, there's
no rule saying you can't play with your food.

Mother bear makes sure each cub gets a piece.

The three bears have always wanted to be close together.
Not now. They don't want to share.

It is harder for mom to keep an eye on them separately
—but she does.

An adult bear might eat eight to ten fish per day, which is equal to
forty hamburgers! Bears have to gorge on salmon when they can.
They will spend the winter in their den, where they don't eat at all.

Sometimes Mom needs a fish to herself.

She must make sure she has energy to keep fishing.

The three bears will always come running
—or climbing—to get whatever they can.

Little One seems to be first for adventure
but last for food.

All of a sudden there's a ruckus.

The bears look to see.

There are five different kinds of salmon, and each has two names. The biggest is called king (chinook), then silver (coho), dog (chum), red (sockeye), and pink (humpy).

It's three BIG bears having a BIG argument.

The three little bears stand up to see.

Male brown bears weigh up to 1,500 pounds along the coast of Alaska, compared to about 500 pounds for grizzlies living in the state's interior. Near the coast bears catch a lot more fish, have more vegetation to eat, and have a milder climate. A milder climate means less time in a den. In Alaska's cold snowy interior, bears may den for seven months. Near Kodiak and other mild coastal areas, some male bears don't den at all..

Three big bears all went for the same fish.

When bears get bigger they don't like to touch
or even want company.

As these three roar and growl, you can see the
tail of the fish that got away.

The three bears do not like this uproar.

Once again, Little One is in front, all three touching as they move out of the way.

Mom doesn't like all the commotion either.

She leads her cubs to find a quieter place.

The water is deeper here.

A mere wade for Mom is a swim for the cubs.

She stands guard and makes sure they get across.

Adult bears are good swimmers. They spend hours at a time in the water, fishing or just hanging out.

This is more like it—together all alone.

Mother bear shows the cubs another fishing spot.

Maybe it's a place her mom showed her long ago.

The three bears
are lucky to have
tasty fish,
fresh air,
clean rivers,
and wild scenery.

An ecosystem is the relationship between the animals and the area they live in. It includes fish, birds, animals, plants, trees, water, soil, and people. All of the elements of an ecosystem depend on each other to remain in balance. Bears, fish, rivers, and land are equally important parts of the ecosystem along the coasts of Katmai National Park.

These cubs are just nine months old. In a few years they will leave their mother. They may stay with each other, even denning together for a year or two. Eventually they will all go on their own. As adults they will recognize each other and even play and wrestle together at times.

Kids will be kids.

Sometimes they just want to play.

Mom knows the fish won't run forever.

She wants her cubs ready
for the long winter's den.

Someday the three bears will have to catch fish on their own.

Mom gathers all three on the river bank to watch and learn.

Bear fishing techniques may include, waiting at the top of a waterfall, sitting on the bottom pawing around, snorkeling in deep water, or stealing fish from someone else.

So they sit and pay attention.

Mom shows one fishing technique —wait for a splash, then pounce!

Little One edges forward.

"I want to do that," she thinks.

"I can wait for a splash, then pounce."

Inching closer and closer
to the water,
Little One
looks less
like a bear
and more
like an otter.

Now there's just two.

"Oh, here's a feather!"

The brothers start to play.

"Weren't there three just a minute ago?"

Big One looks high.

Middle One looks low.

They stand up to look over the grass.

"Down the river she goes
—without you and me!"

Cubs like to stand up so they can see better. Adult bears stand up for the same reason, though it's often misunderstood as a sign of aggression.

"I'll catch my own fish, one just for me."

Jumping and pouncing
   she chases shadows and splashes
      for a long way downstream,
         only to discover that fish
            are elusive and slippery.

She stops on a rock to rest and recover.

She was so focused on fishing, Little One
didn't realize how tired she had become.

"Where are mother bear and my brothers?"

"Mama," she cries.

"I'm here all alone."

It's a bit of a mystery.

How do moms know just where to look?

Mother bear leads her cub back.

Elated to see Mom, Little One follows
sheepishly.

Back upriver they go.

How did she get so far?

Those fish led her on a
wild goose chase!

Both brothers were good and waited on
the river bank.

Now they're relieved to see Mom with
Little One in tow.

Little One is back and tells them all about it.

"Those fish are hard to catch.

We have lots to learn to get as good as Mom."

Mom resumes the search for fish with the three bears all back by her side.

Maybe the cubs can't catch fish yet, but they can help by looking for leftovers.

Bears have a keen sense of smell, even better than a dog. Besides fish, they eat berries, grass, roots, ground squirrels, and sometimes larger animals if they can catch them. Some coastal bears have even learned how to dig for clams.

There was so much excitement today that
the three bears are getting sleepy.

Now it's time for a nap.

Snuggled together, the three bears find a sun-warmed beach where the river meets the sea.

Already another lesson, this time about rising tides.

Soon the water crowds their napping spot.

Their nap is cut short.

The three bears are still weary.

An estuary is the zone where a river meets the sea. When the tide rises, the river becomes shorter. When the tide goes out, the river becomes longer. Bears like estuaries because fish naturally concentrate there.

Even Mom is running out of steam.

Fishing is slow.

The shadows are getting long.

Fog begins to settle in.

Bears enter a winter den not because of the cold but due to lack of available food. So they sleep through the winter. Body temperature, heart rate, and breathing slows down. They do not eat or drink or even go to the bathroom. Bears weigh the least when they emerge from their den in the spring. By then they may have lost about one-third of their weight.

Now it's time to find a quiet place away from the river for the night.

The three bears cross the river one last time.

What will happen tomorrow?

We'll just wait and see.

For the three bears tonight,
sweet dreams might include
rivers, having fun, getting lost, and good food.

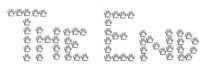